The Stream &
the Sapphire

BOOKS BY DENISE LEVERTOV

Poetry
The Double Image
Here and Now
Overland to the Islands
With Eyes at the Back of Our Heads
The Jacob's Ladder
O Taste and See
The Sorrow Dance
Relearning the Alphabet
To Stay Alive
Footprints
The Freeing of the Dust
Life in the Forest
Collected Earlier Poems 1940–1960
Candles in Babylon
Poems 1960–1967
Oblique Prayers
Poems 1968–1972
Breathing the Water
A Door in the Hive
Evening Train
Sands of the Well
The Life Around Us
The Stream and the Sapphire
This Great Unknowing: Last Poems

Prose
New & Selected Essays
Tesserae: Memories & Suppositions
The Letters of Denise Levertov & William Carlos Williams

Translations
Guillevic/Selected Poems
Joubert/Black Iris (Copper Canyon Press)

DENISE LEVERTOV

The Stream &
the Sapphire

SELECTED POEMS
ON RELIGIOUS THEMES

A New Directions Book

The Stream and the Sapphire incorporates poems from seven previous Denise Levertov books with New Directions: *The Sands of the Well* (1996), *Evening Train* (1992), *A Door in the Hive* (1989), *Breathing the Water* (1987), *Oblique Prayers* (1984), *Candles in Babylon* (1982), and *Life in the Forest* (1978).

Designed by Sylvia Frezzolini Severance
Manufactured in the United States of America
New Directions Books are printed on acid-free paper
First published clothbound and as New Directions Paperbook 844 in 1997
Published simultaneously in Canada by Penguin Books Canada Limited

Library of Congress Cataloging in Publication Data

Levertov, Denise, 1923–
   The stream and the sapphire : selected poems on religious themes /
Denise Levertov.
     p. cm.
   ISBN 0–8112–1353–6 (cloth : alk. paper). — ISBN 978-0-8112-1354-7
(paperbook : alk. paper)
   1. Religious poetry, American.   I. Title.
PS3562.E8876A6   1997
811'.54—dc21   96–30012
                                                                    CIP

New Directions Books are published for James Laughlin
by New Directions Publishing Corporation
80 Eighth Avenue, New York 10011

TENTH PRINTING

Contents

Foreword

Included here are poems from seven separate volumes, the
earliest dating from 1978; and although the sequence is not
wholly chronological it does, to some extent, trace my own
slow movement from agnosticism to Christian faith, a move-
ment incorporating much of doubt and questioning as well as
of affirmation. Other poems imagine historical personages
(e.g. St. Peter, Caedmon, Brother Lawrence) or with some
temerity attempt to enter as deeply as I could into crucial
events of the New Testament. This enterprise in what I think
of as do-it-yourself theology seemed at the time of writing to
risk presumption, but I later discovered it was much like
what Ignatius of Loyola recommended in the 'Exercises.'

The raison d'être for such a selection, along with a com-
panion volume of 'nature' or 'ecologically concerned' poems is
a demand from quite a few readers for a compact thematic
grouping of poems which were originally published in various
separate books. I don't really like segregating poems, and
there are so many (mine and others') which overlap in theme
or resist all categorization; yet I have to acknowledge that
when reading on somewhat specialized occasions (e.g. at a
rally for some peace and justice cause, or to a group of ecolo-
gists, or at a spiritual retreat) I have picked out the poems
which seemed most relevant—and to do so has involved in-

convenient hopping from book to book. This volume is conceived, then, as a convenience to those readers who are themselves concerned with doubt and faith and, though they read a wide variety of poems, like to have a focussed single volume at times, to stuff in a pocket or place at their bedside.

—Denise Levertov

PART ONE

The Tide

Human being—walking
in doubt from childhood on: walking

a ledge of slippery stone in the world's woods
deep-layered with wet leaves—rich or sad: on one
side of the path, ecstasy, on the other
dull grief.   Walking

the mind's imperial cities, roofed-over alleys,
                              thoroughfares, wide boulevards
that hold evening primrose of sky in steady calipers.

Always the mind
walking, working, stopping sometimes to kneel
in awe of beauty, sometimes leaping, filled with the energy
of delight, but never able to pass
the wall, the wall
of brick that crumbles and is replaced,
of twisted iron,
of rock,
the wall that speaks, saying monotonously:

          Children and animals
                              who cannot learn
          anything from suffering,

suffer, are tortured, die
in incomprehension.

This human being, each night nevertheless
summoning—with a breath blown at a flame,
                                    or hand's touch
on the lamp-switch—darkness,
                            silently utters,
impelled as if by a need to cup the palms
and drink from a river,
                    the words, 'Thanks.
Thanks for this day, a day of my life.'
                                And wonders.
Pulls up the blankets, looking
into nowhere, always in doubt.
And takes strange pleasure
in having repeated once more the childish formula,
a pleasure in what is seemly.
And drifts to sleep, downstream
on murmuring currents of doubt and praise,
the wall shadowy, that tomorrow
will cast its own familiar, chill, clear-cut shadow
into the day's brilliance.

I know this happiness
is provisional:

> the looming presences—
> great suffering, great fear—

> withdraw only
> into peripheral vision:

but ineluctable this shimmering
of wind in the blue leaves:

this flood of stillness
widening the lake of sky:

this need to dance,
this need to kneel:
> this mystery:

The Avowal

*For Carolyn Kizer and John Woodbridge,
Recalling Our Celebration
of George Herbert's Birthday, 1983*

As swimmers dare
to lie face to the sky
and water bears them,
as hawks rest upon air
and air sustains them,
so would I learn to attain
freefall, and float
into Creator Spirit's deep embrace,
knowing no effort earns
that all-surrounding grace.

'The Holy One, blessed be he, wanders again,'
said Jacob, 'He is wandering and
looks for a place where he can rest.'

Between the pages
a wren's feather
to mark what passage?
Blood, not dry,
beaded scarlet on dusty stones.
A look of wonder
barely perceived on a turning face —
what, who had they seen?
Traces.
Here's the cold inn,
the wanderer passed it by
searching once more
for a stable's warmth,
a birthplace.

And the secret names
of all we meet who lead us deeper
into our labyrinth
of valleys and mountains, twisting valleys
and steeper mountains—
their hidden names are always,
like Proverb, promises:
Rune, Omen, Fable, Parable,
those we meet for only
one crucial moment, gaze to gaze,
or for years know and don't recognize

but of whom later a word
sings back to us
as if from high among leaves,
still near but beyond sight

drawing us from tree to tree
towards the time and the unknown place
where we shall know
what it is to arrive.

Where the stone steps
falter and come to an end
but the hillside rises
yet more steeply,
obtruded roots of the pines
have braided themselves
across the path to continue
the zigzag staircase.
In times past the non-human—
plants, animals—
often, with such gestures,
intervened in our lives,
or so our forebears
believed when all lives were seen
as travellings-forth of souls.
One can perceive
few come here now—
it's nothing special,
not even very old,
a naive piety,
artless, narrow. And yet
this ladder of roots
draws one onward, coaxing
feet to become
pilgrim feet, that climb
(silenced by layers

of fallen needles,
but step by step
held from sliding)
up to the last
cross of the calvary.

With certitude
Simeon opened
ancient arms
to infant light.
Decades
before the cross, the tomb
and the new life,
he knew
new life.
What depth
of faith he drew on,
turning illumined
towards deep night.

Given that lambs
are infant sheep, that sheep
are afraid and foolish, and lack
the means of self-protection, having
neither rage nor claws,
venom nor cunning,
what then
is this 'Lamb of God'?

This pretty creature, vigorous
to nuzzle at milky dugs,
woolbearer, bleater,
leaper in air for delight of being, who finds in astonishment
four legs to land on, the grass
all it knows of the world?
          With whom we would like to play,
whom we'd lead with ribbons, but may not bring
into our houses because
it would soil the floor with its droppings?

What terror lies concealed
in strangest words, *O lamb*
of God that taketh away

the Sins of the World: an innocence
                    smelling of ignorance,
                    born in bloody snowdrifts,
                    licked by forebearing
dogs more intelligent than its entire flock put together?

                              God then,
                encompassing all things, is
                defenseless? Omnipotence
                has been tossed away, reduced
                to a wisp of damp wool?

                         And we
                frightened, bored, wanting
only to sleep till catastrophe
has raged, clashed, seethed and gone by without us,
                         wanting then
to awaken in quietude without remembrance of agony,

                    we who in shamefaced private hope
                    had looked to be plucked from fire and given
                    a bliss we deserved for having imagined it,

                    is it implied that *we*
                    must protect this perversely weak
                    animal, whose muzzle's nudgings

suppose there is milk to be found in us?
Must hold to our icy hearts
a shivering God?

•

So be it.
            Come, rag of pungent
quiverings,
                dim star.
                            Let's try
            if something human still
            can shield you,
                                spark
            of remote light.

Lord, not you,
it is I who am absent.
At first
belief was a joy I kept in secret,
stealing alone
into sacred places:
a quick glance, and away — and back,
circling.
I have long since uttered your name
but now
I elude your presence.
I stop
to think about you, and my mind
at once
like a minnow darts away,
darts
into the shadows, into gleams that fret
unceasing over
the river's purling and passing.
Not for one second
will my self hold still, but wanders
anywhere,
everywhere it can turn. Not you,
it is I am absent.
You are the stream, the fish, the light,
the pulsing shadow,

you the unchanging presence, in whom all
moves and changes.
How can I focus my flickering, perceive
at the fountain's heart
the sapphire I know is there?

'Adam, where are you?'
                God's hands
palpate darkness, the void
that is Adam's inattention,
his confused attention to everything,
impassioned by multiplicity, his despair.

Multiplicity, his despair;
                God's hands
enacting blindness. Like a child
at a barbaric fairgrounds—
noise, lights, the violent odors—
Adam fragments himself. The whirling rides!

Fragmented Adam stares.
                God's hands
unseen, the whirling rides
dazzle, the lights blind him. Fragmented,
he is not present to himself. God
suffers the void that is his absence.

Assail God's hearing with gull-screech knifeblades.

Cozen the saints to plead our cause, claiming
grace abounding.

God crucified on the resolve not to displume
our unused wings

hears: nailed palms
cannot beat off the flames of insistent sound,

strident or plaintive,
nor reach to annul freedom—

nor would God renege.

Our shoulders ache. The abyss
gapes at us.

When shall we
dare to fly?

It's when we face for a moment
the worst our kind can do, and shudder to know
the taint in our own selves, that awe
cracks the mind's shell and enters the heart:
not to a flower, not to a dolphin,
to no innocent form
but to this creature vainly sure
it and no other is god-like, God
(out of compassion for our ugly
failure to evolve) entrusts,
as guest, as brother,
the Word.

Variation on a Theme by Rilke

(*The Book of Hours*, Book I, Poem 4)

All these images (said the old monk,
closing the book) these inspired depictions,
are true. Yes—not one—Giotto's,
Van Eyck's, Rembrandt's, Rouault's,
how many others'—
not one is a fancy, a willed fiction,
each of them shows us exactly
the manifold countenance
of the Holy One, Blessed be He.
The seraph buttress flying
to support a cathedral's external walls,
the shadowy ribs of the vaulted sanctuary:
aren't both—and equally—
the form of a holy place?—whose windows' ruby
and celestial sapphire can be seen
only from inside, but then
only when light enters from without?
From the divine twilight, neither dark nor day,
blossoms the morning. Each, at work in his art,
perceived his neighbor. Thus the Infinite
plays, and in grace
gives us clues to His mystery.

Psalm Fragments (Schnittke String Trio)

This clinging to a God
for whom one does
nothing.
        A loyalty
without deeds.

          •

Tyrant God.
Cruel God.
Heartless God.

God who permits
the endless outrage we call
History.

Deaf God.
Blind God.
Idiot God.

(Scapegoat god. Finally
running out of accusations
we deny Your existence.)

•

I don't forget
that downhill street
of spilled garbage and beat-up cars,
the gray faces
looking up, all color
gone with the sun —

disconsolate, prosaic twilight
at midday. And the fear
of blindness.

It's harder to recall
the relief when plain
daylight returned

subtly, softly,
without the fuss
of trumpets.
                    Yet
our faces had been upturned
like those of gazers
into a sky of angels
at Birth or Ascension.

•

Lord, I curl in Thy grey
gossamer hammock

that swings by one
elastic thread to thin
twigs that could, that should
break but don't.

.

I do nothing, I give You
nothing. Yet You hold me

minute by minute
from falling.

Lord, You provide.

I had grasped God's garment in the void
but my hand slipped
on the rich silk of it.
The 'everlasting arms' my sister loved to remember
must have upheld my leaden weight
from falling, even so,
for though I claw at empty air and feel
nothing, no embrace,
I have not plummetted.

Where is the Giver to whom my gratitude
rose? In this emptiness
there seems no Presence.

·

How confidently the desires
of God are spoken of!
Perhaps God wants
something quite different.
Or nothing, nothing at all.

·

Blue smoke from small
peaceable hearths ascending
without resistance in luminous
evening air.
Or eager mornings—waking
as if to a song's call.
Easily I can conjure
a myriad images
of faith.
Remote. They pass
as I turn a page.

•

Outlying houses, and the train's rhythm
slows, there's a signal box,
people are taking their luggage
down from the racks.
Then you wake and discover
you have not left
to begin the journey.

•

Faith's a tide, it seems, ebbs and flows responsive
to action and inaction.
Remain in stasis, blown sand
stings your face, anemones
shrivel in rock pools no wave renews.
Clean the littered beach, clear
the lines of a forming poem,
the waters flood inward.
Dull stones again fulfill
their glowing destinies, and emptiness
is a cup, and holds
the ocean.

Birds afloat in air's current,
sacred breath? No, not breath of God,
it seems, but God
the air enveloping the whole
globe of being.
It's we who breathe, in, out, in, the sacred,
leaves astir, our wings
rising, ruffled — but only the saints
take flight. We cower
in cliff-crevice or edge out gingerly
on branches close to the nest. The wind
marks the passage of holy ones riding
that ocean of air. Slowly their wake
reaches us, rocks us.
But storm or still,
numb or poised in attention,
we inhale, exhale, inhale,
encompassed, encompassed.

The Beginning of Wisdom

Proverbs 9.–10

You have brought me so far.

.

I know so much. Names, verbs, images. My mind
overflows, a drawer that can't close.

.

Unscathed among the tortured. Ignorant parchment
uninscribed, light strokes only, where a scribe
tried out a pen.

.

I am so small, a speck of dust
moving across the huge world. The world
a speck of dust in the universe.

.

Are you holding
the universe? You hold
onto my smallness. How do you grasp it,

how does it not
slip away?

•

I know so little.

•

You have brought me so far.

1

Again before your altar, silent Lord.
And here the sound of rushing waters,
a dove's crooning.

Not every temple serves
as your resting-place.
Here, though, today,
over the river's continuo,
under the dove's soliloquy,
your hospitable silence.

2

Again before thy altar, silent Lord.

Thy presence is made known
by untraced interventions
like those legendary baskets filled
with bread and wine, discovered
at the door by someone at wit's end
returning home empty-handed
after a day of looking for work.

To lie back under the tallest
oldest trees. How far the stems
rise, rise
        before ribs of shelter
                open!

To live in the mercy of God. The complete
sentence too adequate, has no give.
Awe, not comfort. Stone, elbows of
stony wood beneath lenient
moss bed.

And awe suddenly
passing beyond itself. Becomes
a form of comfort.
                Becomes the steady
        air you glide on, arms
stretched like the wings of flying foxes.
To hear the multiple silence
of trees, the rainy
forest depths of their listening.

To float, upheld,
        as salt water

31

would hold you,
                              once you dared.

          •

To live in the mercy of God.

To feel vibrate the enraptured

          waterfall flinging itself
          unabating down and down
                              to clenched fists of rock.
          Swiftness of plunge,
          hour after year after century,
                              O or Ah
          uninterrupted, voice
          many-stranded.
                              To breathe
          spray. The smoke of it.
                              Arcs
          of steelwhite foam, glissades
          of fugitive jade barely perceptible. Such passion —
          rage or joy?
                              Thus, not mild, not temperate,
          God's love for the world. Vast
          flood of mercy
                    flung on resistance.

Days pass when I forget the mystery.
Problems insoluble and problems offering
their own ignored solutions
jostle for my attention, they crowd its antechamber
along with a host of diversions, my courtiers, wearing
their colored clothes; cap and bells.
                And then
once more the quiet mystery
is present to me, the throng's clamor
recedes: the mystery
that there is anything, anything at all,
let alone cosmos, joy, memory, everything,
rather than void: and that, O Lord,
Creator, Hallowed One, You still,
hour by hour sustain it.

PART TWO

Believers

'Straight to the point'
        can ricochet,
                unconvincing.
Circumlocution, analogy,
        parable's ambiguities, provide
                context, stepping-stones.

Most of the time. And then

the lightning power
        amidst these indirections,
                of plain
unheralded miracle!
        For example,
                as if forgetting
to prepare them, He simply
        walks on water
                toward them, casually—
and impetuous Peter, empowered,
        jumps from the boat and rushes
                on wave-tip to meet Him—
a few steps, anyway—
        (till it occurs to him,
                'I can't, this is preposterous'
and Jesus has to grab him,
        tumble his weight

back over the gunwale).
Sustaining those light and swift
         steps was more than Peter
                  could manage. Still,
years later,
         his toes and insteps, just before sleep,
                  would remember their passage.

Delivered out of raw continual pain,
smell of darkness, groans of those others
to whom he was chained—

unchained, and led
past the sleepers,
door after door silently opening—
out!
     And along a long street's
majestic emptiness under the moon:

one hand on the angel's shoulder, one
feeling the air before him,
eyes open but fixed . . .

And not till he saw the angel had left him,
alone and free to resume
the ecstatic, dangerous, wearisome roads of
what he had still to do,
not till then did he recognize
this was no dream. More frightening
than arrest, than being chained to his warders:
he could hear his own footsteps suddenly.
Had the angel's feet

made any sound? He could not recall.
No one had missed him, no one was in pursuit.
He himself must be
the key, now, to the next door,
the next terrors of freedom and joy.

All others talked as if
talk were a dance.
Clodhopper I, with clumsy feet
would break the gliding ring.
Early I learned to
hunch myself
close by the door:
then when the talk began
I'd wipe my
mouth and wend
unnoticed back to the barn
to be with the warm beasts,
dumb among body sounds
of the simple ones.
I'd see by a twist
of lit rush the motes
of gold moving
from shadow to shadow
slow in the wake
of deep untroubled sighs.
The cows
munched or stirred or were still. I
was at home and lonely,
both in good measure. Until
the sudden angel affrighted me—light effacing
my feeble beam,

a forest of torches, feathers of flame, sparks upflying:
but the cows as before
were calm, and nothing was burning,
            nothing but I, as that hand of fire
touched my lips and scorched my tongue
and pulled my voice
                    into the ring of the dance.

The Servant-Girl at Emmaus
(A Painting by Velázquez)

She listens, listens, holding
her breath. Surely that voice
is his—the one
who had looked at her, once, across the crowd,
as no one ever had looked?
Had seen her? Had spoken as if to her?

Surely those hands were his,
taking the platter of bread from hers just now?
Hands he'd laid on the dying and made them well?

Surely that face—?

The man they'd crucified for sedition and blasphemy.
The man whose body disappeared from its tomb.
The man it was rumored now some women had seen this
                                    morning, alive?

Those who had brought this stranger home to their table
don't recognize yet with whom they sit.
But she in the kitchen, absently touching

                              the winejug she's to take in,
a young Black servant intently listening,

swings round and sees
the light around him
and is sure.

Conversion of Brother Lawrence

'Let us enter into ourselves,
Time presses.
Brother Lawrence 1611–1691

1

What leafless tree plunging
into what pent sky was it
convinced you Spring, bound to return
in all its unlikelihood, was a word
of God, a Divine message?
Custom, natural reason, are everyone's assurance;
we take the daylight for granted, the moon,
the measured tides. A particular tree, though,
one day in your eighteenth winter,
said more, an oracle. Clumsy footman,
apt to drop the ornate objects handed to you,
cursed and cuffed by butlers and grooms,
your inner life unsuspected,
you heard, that day, a more-than-green
voice from the stripped branches.
Wooden lace, a celestial geometry, uttered
more than familiar rhythms of growth.
It said *By the Grace of God.*
Midsummer rustled around you that wintry moment.
Was it elm, ash, poplar, a fruit-tree, your rooted
twig-winged angel of annunciation?

Out from the chateau park it sent you
(by some back lane, no doubt,
not through the wide gates of curled iron),
by ways untold, by soldier's marches, to the obscure
clatter and heat of a monastery kitchen,
a broom's rhythmic whisper for music,
your torment the drudgery of household ledgers. Destiny
without visible glory. 'Time pressed.' Among pots and pans,
heart-still through the bustle of chores,
your labors, hard as the pain in your lame leg,
grew slowly easier over the years, the years
when, though your soul felt darkened, heavy, worthless,
yet God, you discovered, never abandoned you but walked
at your side keeping pace as comrades had
on the long hard roads of war. You entered then
the unending 'silent secret conversation,'
the life of steadfast attention.
Not work transformed you; work, even drudgery,
was transformed: that discourse
pierced through its monotones, infused them
with streams of sparkling color.
What needed doing, you did; journeyed if need be
on rocking boats, lame though you were,
to the vineyard country to purchase the year's wine
for a hundred Brothers, laughably rolling yourself
over the deck-stacked barrels when you couldn't
keep your footing; and managed deals with the vintners

to your own surprise, though business was nothing to you.
Your secret was not the craftsman's delight in process,
which doesn't distinguish work from pleasure—
your way was not to exalt nor avoid
the Adamic legacy, you simply made it irrelevant:
everything faded, thinned to nothing, beside
the light which bathed and warmed, the Presence
your being had opened to. Where it shone,
there life was, and abundantly; it touched
your dullest task, and the task was easy.
                    Joyful, absorbed,
you 'practiced the presence of God' as a musician
practices hour after hour his art:
'A stone before the carver,'
you 'entered into yourself.'

Dom Helder, octogenarian wisp
of human substance arrived from Brazil,
raises his arms and gazes toward
a sky pallid with heat, to implore
'Peace!'
          —then waves a 'goodbye for now'
to God, as to a *compadre*.
'The Mass is over, go in peace
to love and serve the Lord': he walks
down with the rest of us to cross
the cattle-grid, entering forbidden ground
where marshals wait with their handcuffs.

After hours of waiting,
penned into two wire-fenced enclosures, sun
climbing to cloudless zenith, till everyone
has been processed, booked, released to trudge
one by one up the slope to the boundary line
back to a freedom that's not so free,
we are all reassembled. We form
two circles, one contained in the other, to dance
clockwise and counterclockwise
like children in Duncan's vision.
But not to the song of ashes, of falling:
we dance in the unity that brought us here,

instinct pulls us into the ancient
rotation, symbol of continuance.
Light and persistent as tumbleweed,
but not adrift, Dom Helder, too,
faithful pilgrim, dances,
dances at the turning core.

The Showings: Lady Julian of Norwich,
1342–1416

1

Julian, there are vast gaps we call black holes,
unable to picture what's both dense and vacant;

and there's the dizzying multiplication of all
language can name or fail to name, unutterable
swarming of molecules. All Pascal
imagined he could not stretch his mind to imagine
is known to exceed his dread.

And there's the earth of our daily history,
its memories, its present filled with the grain
of one particular scrap of carpentered wood we happen
to be next to, its waking light on one especial leaf,
this word or that, a tune in this key not another,
beat of our hearts *now*, good or bad,
dying or being born, eroded, vanishing—

And you ask us to turn our gaze
inside out, and see
a little thing, the size of a hazelnut, and believe
it is our world? Ask us to see it lying

in God's pierced palm? That it encompasses
every awareness our minds contain? All Time?
All limitless space given form in this
medieval enigma?
                         Yes, this is indeed
what you ask, sharing
the mystery you were shown: *all that is made:*
a little thing, the size of a hazelnut, held safe
in God's pierced palm.

2

What she petitioned for was never
instead of something else.
Thirty was older than it is now. She had not married
but was no starveling; if she had loved,
she had been loved. Death or some other destiny
bore him away, death or some other bride
changed him. Whatever that story,
long since she had travelled
through and beyond it. Somehow,
reading or read to, she'd spiralled
up within tall towers
of learning, steeples of discourse.
Bells in her spirit
rang new changes.
                    Swept beyond event, one longing
outstripped all others: that reality,
supreme reality,
be witnessed. To desire wounds—
three, no less, no more—
is audacity, not, five centuries early, neurosis;
it's the desire to enact metaphor, for flesh to make known
to intellect (as uttered song
                makes known to voice,
                as image to eye)
make known in bone and breath
(and not die) God's agony.

3

'To understand her, you must imagine . . .'
A childhood, then;
the dairy's bowls of clabber, of rich cream,
ghost-white in shade, and outside
the midsummer gold, humming of dandelions.
To run back and forth, into the chill again,
the sweat of slate, a cake of butter
set on a green leaf—out once more
over slab of stone into hot light, hot
wood, the swinging gate!
A spire we think ancient split the blue
between two trees, a half-century old—
she thought it ancient.
Her father's hall, her mother's bower,
nothing was dull. The cuckoo
was changing its tune. In the church
there was glass in the windows, glass
colored like the world. You could see
Christ and his mother and his cross,
you could see his blood, and the throne of God.
In the fields
calves were lowing, the shepherd was taking the sheep
to new pasture.
            Julian perhaps
not yet her name, this child's
that vivid woman.

4

God's wounded hand
reached out to place in hers
the entire world, 'round as a ball,
small as a hazelnut.' Just so one day
of infant light remembered
her mother might have given
into her two cupped palms
a newlaid egg, warm from the hen;
just so her brother
risked to her solemn joy
his delicate treasure,
a sparrow's egg from the hedgerow.
What can this be? *the eye of her understanding* marveled.

God for a moment in our history
placed in that five-fingered
human nest
the macrocosmic egg, sublime paradox,
brown hazelnut of All that Is—
made, and belov'd, and preserved.
As still, waking each day within
our microcosm, we find it, and ourselves.

Why did she laugh?
In scorn of malice.

What did they think?
They thought she was dying.

They caught her laugh?
Even the priest—

the dark small room
quivered with merriment,

all unaccountably
lightened.

If they had known
what she was seeing—

> the very
> spirit of evil,

> the Fiend they dreaded,
> seen to be oafish, ridiculous, vanquished—

what amazement! Stupid,
stupid his mar-plot malevolence!

Silly as his horns and
imaginary tail!

Why did her laughter
stop? Her mind moved on:

      the cost, the cost,
      the passion it took to undo

      the deeds of malice.
      The deathly

      wounds and the anguished
      heart.
And they?

They were abashed,
stranded in hilarity.

But when she recovered,
they told one another:

'Remember how we laughed
without knowing why?
That was the turning-point!'

6

Julian laughing aloud, glad
with *a most high inward happiness,*

Julian open calmly to dismissive judgments
flung backward down the centuries—
'delirium,' 'hallucination';

Julian walking underwater
on the green hills of moss, the detailed sand and seaweed,
pilgrim of the depths, unfearing;

twenty years later carefully retelling
each unfading vision, each
pondered understanding;

Julian of whom we know
she had two serving-maids, Alice and Sara,
and kept a cat, and looked God in the face
and lived—

Julian nevertheless
said that *deeds are done so evil, injuries inflicted
so great, it seems to us
impossible any good
can come of them—*

any redemption, then, transform them . . .

She lived in dark times, as we do:
war, and the Black Death, hunger, strife,
torture, massacre. She knew
all of this, she felt it
sorrowfully, mournfully,
shaken as men shake
a cloth in the wind.
                    But Julian, Julian—
I turn to you:
                    you clung to joy though tears and sweat
rolled down your face like the blood
you watched pour down *in beads uncountable*
as rain from the eaves:
clung like an acrobat, by your teeth, fiercely,
to a cobweb-thin high-wire, your certainty
of infinite mercy, witnessed
with your own eyes, with outward sight
in your small room, with inward sight
in your untrammeled spirit—
knowledge we long to share:
Love was his meaning.

Annunciatión

'Hail, space for the uncontained God'
From the Agathistos Hymn,
Greece, VIc

We know the scene: the room, variously furnished,
almost always a lectern, a book; always
the tall lily.
　　　　Arrived on solemn grandeur of great wings,
the angelic ambassador, standing or hovering,
whom she acknowledges, a guest.

But we are told of meek obedience. No one mentions
courage.
　　　　The engendering Spirit
did not enter her without consent.
　　　　　　　　　God waited.

She was free
to accept or to refuse, choice
integral to humanness.

———————————

Aren't there annunciations
of one sort or another

in most lives?
                    Some unwillingly
undertake great destinies,
enact them in sullen pride,
uncomprehending.
                    More often
those moments
        when roads of light and storm
        open from darkness in a man or woman,
are turned away from
in dread, in a wave of weakness, in despair
and with relief.
Ordinary lives continue.
                            God does not smite them.
But the gates close, the pathway vanishes.

———————————

She had been a child who played, ate, slept
like any other child—but unlike others,
wept only for pity, laughed
in joy not triumph.
Compassion and intelligence
fused in her, indivisible.

Called to a destiny more momentous
than any in all of Time,
she did not quail,
                    only asked

a simple, 'How can this be?'
and gravely, courteously,
took to heart the angel's reply,
perceiving instantly
the astounding ministry she was offered:

to bear in her womb
Infinite weight and lightness; to carry
in hidden, finite inwardness,
nine months of Eternity; to contain
in slender vase of being,
the sum of power—
in narrow flesh,
the sum of light.
           Then bring to birth,
push out into air, a Man-child
needing, like any other,
milk and love—

but who was God.

PART THREE

Conjectures

On the Parables of the Mustard Seed

(*Matthew 17.20, Mark 4.30–32,
Luke 13.18–19*)

Who ever saw the mustard-plant,
wayside weed or tended crop,
grow tall as a shrub, let alone a tree, a treeful
of shade and nests and songs?
Acres of yellow,
not a bird of the air in sight.

No, He who knew
the west wind brings
the rain, the south wind
thunder, who walked the field-paths
running His hand along wheatstems to glean
those intimate milky kernels, good
to break on the tongue,

was talking of miracle, the seed
within us, so small
we take it for worthless, a mustard-seed, dust,
nothing.
　　　　Glib generations mistake
the metaphor, not looking at fields and trees,

not noticing paradox. Mountains
remain unmoved.

Faith is rare, He must have been saying,
prodigious, unique —
one infinitesimal grain divided
like loaves and fishes,

as if from a mustard-seed
a great shade-tree grew. That rare,
that strange: the kingdom

                a tree. The soul
a bird. A great concourse of birds
at home there, wings among yellow flowers.
The waiting
kingdom of faith, the seed
waiting to be sown.

Literal minds! Embarrassed humans! His friends
were blushing for Him
in secret; wouldn't admit they were shocked.
They thought Him
petulant to curse me! —yet how could the Lord
be unfair? —so they looked away,
then and now.
But I, I knew that
helplessly barren though I was,
my day had come. I served
Christ the Poet,
who spoke in images: I was at hand,
a metaphor for their failure to bring forth
what is within them (as figs
were *not* within me). They who had walked
in His sunlight presence,
they could have ripened,
could have perceived His thirst and hunger,
His innocent appetite;
they could have offered
human fruits—compassion, comprehension—
without being asked,
without being told of need.
My absent fruit

stood for their barren hearts. He cursed
not me, not them, but
(ears that hear not, eyes that see not)
their dullness, that withholds
gifts *unimagined*.

When God makes dust of our cooling magma,
musingly crumbling the last
galls and studs of our being,

the only place we can go if we're not
destined for hell, or there already,
is purgatory—for certainly heaven's
no place for a film of dust to settle;

and I see no reason why purgatory
may not be reincarnation, the soul
passing from human to another
earth-form more innocent—even to try

the human again, ablaze
with outsetting infant wonder—from which
to learn, as expiation progressed,
neglected tasks.
            Then

the sifting again, between thoughtful fingers,
the rubbing to finer substance.
                  Then perhaps

time for the floating
                   into light,
                         to rest suspended
                         mote by silvery mote
                   in that bright veil to await
the common resurrection.

PART FOUR

Fish and a Honeycomb

Maybe He looked indeed
much as Rembrandt envisioned Him
in those small heads that seem in fact
portraits of more than a model.
A dark, still young, very intelligent face,
a soul-mirror gaze of deep understanding, unjudging.
That face, in extremis, would have clenched its teeth
in a grimace not shown in even the great crucifixions.
The burden of humanness (I begin to see) exacted from Him
that He taste also the humiliation of dread,
cold sweat of wanting to let the whole thing go,
like any mortal hero out of his depth,
like anyone who has taken a step too far
and wants herself back.
The painters, even the greatest, don't show how,
in the midnight Garden,
or staggering uphill under the weight of the Cross,
He went through with even the human longing
to simply cease, to not be.
Not torture of body,
not the hideous betrayals humans commit
nor the faithless weakness of friends, and surely
not the anticipation of death (not then, in agony's grip)
was Incarnation's heaviest weight,
but this sickened desire to renege,
to step back from what He, Who was God,

had promised Himself, and had entered
time and flesh to enact.
Sublime acceptance, to be absolute, had to have welled
up from those depths where purpose
drifted for mortal moments.

Six hours outstretched in the sun, yes,
hot wood, the nails, blood trickling
into the eyes, yes—
but the thieves on their neighbor crosses
survived till after the soldiers
had come to fracture their legs, or longer.
Why single out this agony? What's
a mere six hours?
Torture then, torture now,
the same, the pain's the same,
immemorial branding iron,
electric prod.
Hasn't a child
dazed in the hospital ward they reserve
for the most abused, known worse?
This air we're breathing,
these very clouds, ephemeral billows
languid upon the sky's
moody ocean, we share
with women and men who've held out
days and weeks on the rack—
and in the ancient dust of the world
what particles
of the long tormented,
what ashes.

But Julian's lucid spirit leapt
to the difference:
perceived why no awe could measure
that brief day's endless length,
why among all the tortured
One only is 'King of Grief.'
The oneing, she saw, *the oneing
with the Godhead* opened Him utterly
to the pain of all minds, all bodies.
—sands of the sea, of the desert—
from first beginning
to last day. The great wonder is
that the human cells of His flesh and bone
didn't explode
when utmost Imagination rose
in that flood of knowledge. Unique
in agony, Infinite strength, Incarnate,
empowered Him to endure
inside of history,
through those hours when He took to Himself
the sum total of anguish and drank
even the lees of that cup:

within the mesh of the web, Himself
woven within it, yet seeing it,
seeing it whole. *Every sorrow and desolation
He saw, and sorrowed in kinship.*

Down through the tomb's inward arch
He has shouldered out into Limbo
to gather them, dazed, from dreamless slumber:
the merciful dead, the prophets,
the innocents just His own age and those
unnumbered others waiting here
unaware, in an endless void He is ending
now, stooping to tug at their hands,
to pull them from their sarcophagi,
dazzled, almost unwilling. Didmas,
neighbor in death, Golgotha dust
still streaked on the dried sweat of his body
no one had washed and anointed, is here,
for sequence is not known in Limbo;
the promise, given from cross to cross
at noon, arches beyond sunset and dawn.
All these He will swiftly lead
to the Paradise road: they are safe.
That done, there must take place that struggle
no human presumes to picture:
living, dying, descending to rescue the just
from shadow, were lesser travails
than this: to break
through earth and stone of the faithless world
back to the cold sepulchre, tearstained
stifling shroud; to break from *them*

back into breath and heartbeat, and walk
the world again, closed into days and weeks again,
wounds of His anguish open, and Spirit
streaming through every cell of flesh
so that if mortal sight could bear
to perceive it, it would be seen
His mortal flesh was lit from within, now,
and aching for home. He must return,
first, in Divine patience, and know
hunger again, and give
to humble friends the joy
of giving Him food—fish and a honeycomb.

Lent 1988

On Belief in the Physical Resurrection of Jesus

It is for all
        'literalists of the imagination,'
                poets or not,
that miracle
            is possible,
                    possible and essential.
Are some intricate minds
                    nourished
                            on concept,
as epiphytes flourish
                high in the canopy?
                            Can they
subsist on the light,
                on the half
                        of metaphor that's not
grounded in dust, grit,
                heavy
                    carnal clay?
Do signs contain and utter,
                    for them
                            all the reality
that they need? Resurrection, for them,
                an internal power, but not
                        a matter of flesh?
For the others,
        of whom I am one,

                    miracles (ultimate need, bread
of iife) are miracles just because
                    people so tuned
                              to the humdrum laws:
gravity, mortality—
                    can't open
                              to symbol's power
unless convinced of its ground,
                              its roots
                                   in bone and blood.
We must feel
          the pulse in the wound
                              to believe
that 'with God
               all things
                    are possible,'
taste
     bread at Emmaus
                    that warm hands
broke and blessed.

In the hot street at noon I saw him
                                                a small man
          gray but vivid, standing forth
                                                beyond the crowd's buzzing
holding in desperate grip his shaking
                                                teethgnashing son,

and thought him my brother.

I heard him cry out, weeping, and speak
                                                those words,
Lord, I believe, help thou
                              mine unbelief,

and knew him
              my twin:

a man whose entire being
                              had knotted itself
into the one tightdrawn question,
                                        Why,
why has this child lost his childhood in suffering,
                              why is this child who will soon be a man
tormented, torn, twisted?
                              Why is he cruelly punished
who has done nothing except be born?

The twin of my birth
                    was not so close
as that man I heard
                    say what my heart
sighed with each beat, my breath silently
                                   cried in and out,
in and out.

After the healing,
                    he, with his wondering
newly peaceful boy, receded;
                              no one
dwells on the gratitude, the astonished joy,
                                     the swift
acceptance and forgetting.
                         I did not follow
to see their changed lives.
                          What I retained
was the flash of kinship.
                        Despite
all that I witnessed,
                    his question remained
my question, throbbed like a stealthy cancer,
                                   known
only to doctor and patient. To others
                              I seemed well enough.

So it was
          that after Golgotha
                              my spirit in secret
lurched in the same convulsed writhings
                                   that tore that child
before he was healed.
                         And after the empty tomb
when they told me He lived, had spoken to Magdalen,
                                             told me_
that though He had passed through the door like a ghost
                              He had breathed on them
the breath of a living man —
                         even then
when hope tried with a flutter of wings
                              to lift me —
still, alone with myself,
                    my heavy cry was the same: *Lord,*
I believe,
        help thou mine unbelief.

I needed
        blood to tell me the truth,
the touch
        of blood. Even
my sight of the dark crust of it
                              round the nailholes
didn't thrust its meaning all the way through
                              to that manifold knot in me

83

that willed to possess all knowledge,

                              refusing to loosen
unless that insistence won

                    the battle I fought with life

But when my hand

                    led by His hand's firm clasp
entered the unhealed wound,

                              my fingers encountering
rib-bone and pulsing heat,

                    what I felt was not
scalding pain, shame for my

                         obstinate need,
but light, light streaming

                    into me, over me, filling the room
as if I had lived till then

                    in a cold cave, and now
coming forth for the first time,

                    the knot that bound me unravelling,
I witnessed

          all things quicken to color, to form,
my question

               not answered but given

                              its part
in a vast unfolding design lit

                    by a risen sun.

Stretching Himself as if again,
        through downpress of dust
                upward, soil giving way
to thread of white, that reaches
        for daylight, to open as green
                leaf that it is . . .
Can Ascension
        not have been
                arduous, almost,
as the return
        from Sheol, and
                back through the tomb
into breath?
        Matter reanimate
                now must relinquish
itself, its
        human cells,
                molecules, five
senses, linear
        vision endured
                as Man —
the sole
        all-encompassing gaze
                resumed now,
Eye of Eternity.
        Relinquished, earth's

                    broken Eden.
Expulsion,
        liberation,
                last
self-enjoined task
        of Incarnation.
                He again
Fathering Himself.
        Seed-case
                splitting.
He again
        Mothering His birth:
                torture and bliss.

Notes

"The Holy One, blessed be he . . ." and "I learned that her name was Proverb," pages 7 and 8: These two poems are part of a series of "Spinoffs," from *Breathing the Water* (1987). They "span off" from photographs by Peter McAfee Brown when I was preparing to write an introduction to his book, *Seasons of Light*. They should not be mistaken for descriptions.

"Candlemas," page 11: This poem draws on a sermon given by Father Benignus at Stanford, Candlemas 1985.

"Agnus Dei," page 12: From *Mass for the Day of St. Thomas Didymus*.

"On a Theme by Thomas Merton," page 17: the theme alluded to is in one of the tapes of informal lectures given at Gethsemane in the 1960s.

"Variation on a Theme by Rilke (*Book of Hours*, Book I, Poem 4)," page 20: Those who read German will be able to see what images and ideas are taken from the original and which are my own.

"Caedmon," page 41: The story comes, of course, from The Venerable Bede's *History of the English Church and People*, but I first read it as a child in John Richard Green's *History of the English People*, 1855. The poem forms a companion piece to "St. Peter and the Angel" in *The Stream & the Sapphire* as well as in *Oblique Prayers*.

"The Servant-Girl at Emmaus," page 43: The painting by Velázquez is in the National Gallery of Ireland, Dublin. Before it was cleaned, the subject was not apparent: only when the figures at table in a room behind her were revealed was her previously ambiguous expression clearly legible as acutely attentive.

"Conversion of Brother Lawrence," page 45: The quotations are from Brother Lawrence's *The Practice of the Presence of God* (available in many editions), and the biographical allusions are based on the original introductions.

"The Showings," page 50: The quotations are taken from the Pelican and the Paulist Press *Classics of Western Spirituality* editions.

"On a Theme from Julian's Chapter XX," page 75: This is from the longer text of Julian of Norwich's *Showings* (or *Revelations*). The quoted lines follow the Grace Warrack transcription (1901). Warrack uses the word "kinship" in her title-heading for the chapter, though in the text itself she says "kindness," thus—as in her Glossary—reminding one of the roots common to both words.